TEST YOUR CAT'S
CREATIVE INTELLIGENCE

EIGHTEEN
EASY-TO-USE
TEST CARDS TO VERIFY
YOUR CAT'S ARTISTIC ABILITY

Ten Speed Press
Berkeley, California

INTRODUCTION

Nobody fully understands why some domestic cats make marks with paint, but the phenomenon has been known to exist for centuries, with the earliest recorded examples of cat marking dating back to Ancient Egypt.

In recent times, cat painting has been explained by biologists as being a form of territorial marking behavior, yet mounting evidence suggests that some cats' marks are aesthetically motivated and should be regarded as genuine works of non-primate art. Already there are several galleries, like the *Phillip Wood Gallery* in Berkeley, California, and *Villa Ichon* in Bremen, Germany, which specialize in the collection, curation, exhibition, and sale of cat art, and scientific organizations such as the Museum of Non-Primate Art (M.O.N.P.A.) regularly research the many facets of feline aesthetics.

While all domestic cats undoubtedly have the ability to make meaningful marks, and often display a creative aptitude with their claws, very few ever become as skilled as Mindle, who has a creative quotient (CQ) of 115, and her kitten Moitle (seen here completing the now well-known *Swinging Swallows,* which sold for $15,000 in 1995). This has a lot to do with our limited human understanding of cats and our consequent reluctance to encourage them to undertake more complex, human-like tasks. So, while the number of internationally recognized cat artists is currently limited to less than a hundred, it must be remembered that all cats are potential artists, and, if we supply them with non-toxic, scented, acrylic paints or suitable surfaces to sculpt, a significant number may well surprise us with interesting work.

Until now, the problem has been to find a simple way of enabling owners to gauge whether their cat is one of the few endowed with a hidden artistic ability. For, once an owner knows his or her pet has a real talent for producing beautiful and potentially valuable works of art, they are willing to proceed with a comprehensive art encouragement program, secure in the knowledge that their efforts are more than likely to bear fruit. M.O.N.P.A.'s test cards not only provide that simple method of quickly identifying the creative cat, but they also help us to understand a uniquely feline perception of our world from which we may derive valuable insights.

M.O.N.P.A.'s TEST CARDS

The Museum of Non-Primate Art (M.O.N.P.A.) is an internationally funded research organization with several branches located throughout the world. Founded in 1976 by the well-known art historian and animal philanthropist, Dr Peter Hansard, M.O.N.P.A.'s initial focus was on elephant painting, spider web design, and bear scratch forms. However, following the 1980 publication of Arthur Mann's ground-breaking research into representational marking by domestic cats, a new division was set up within the museum to concentrate on research into feline aesthetics and undertake the development, preservation, curation, and exhibition of cat art.

In 1984 M.O.N.P.A. established a salon of resident cat artists to enable researchers to study them at work in a controlled environment. To recruit these cats, a set of test cards was developed with the aim of sorting out the creative cats from the non-creative applicants. Development took longer than expected, but, by 1987, 18 cards were in use by museum staff and had been found to be 82% accurate in predicting a cat's creative intelligence. While modern brain activity scans now offer more effective ways of assessing a cat's creative quotient in the laboratory, these cards are still used by many professionals as an initial screening device, not only by breeders wanting to check a cat's artistic potential, but also by art dealers who may need to verify whether a particular cat is capable of the work claimed for it.

In 1994, when *Newsweek* announced in its September 19 issue that cats could paint, it generated such widespread international interest in cat art that M.O.N.P.A. was swamped with requests for more information from cat owners around the world. In order to handle the demand, the museum set up an interactive Internet site (http://www.netlink.co.nz/~monpa/), which included four of the test cards. Owners could hold their cats up to the computer screen and, judging by the cats' reactions to the images on the cards, determine something of their artistic ability. The cards proved so popular that M.O.N.P.A. decided to publish the full set in this easy-to-use book format in the hope that it would enable many more creatively intelligent cats to be identified and encouraged.

By holding each card very still in front of the cat's face and carefully noting its reactions, the owner is able to determine his pet's level of creative intelligence. In this case, the cat is showing a high degree of aesthetic awareness by touching the more attractive lower image while also curling her tail into the "interested" form.

How To Use The Cards

It is important to remember that these test cards were designed to be used in a laboratory situation, and, while it is difficult to replicate that highly regulated environment in the home, they are most effective when treated as a scientific tool and used under conditions which are as controlled as possible. Here are some suggestions which will help you achieve that control and ensure a credible assessment of your cat's artistic potential.

1. Try to ensure that the test environment is free of all possible distractions. Turn off radios, TVs and other electrical appliances including refrigerators, as cats are very sensitive to even small amounts of static electricity. Natural light is preferable for testing but make sure your cat is unlikely to be distracted by movement outside the window. Noise, smells, and air movements should all be kept to a minimum to avoid inconclusive readings. Ask other people in the house to keep their voices low and avoid unnecessary movement – and don't forget to take the phone off the hook.

2. Except where specifically indicated, the book should be folded in half and just the relevant image held as still as possible in front of the cat's face. Holding the book like this will require the presenter to adopt rather unnatural positions for up to two minutes at a time. These positions should be practiced in front of a mirror before the actual presentation is made in order to check that the card can be held with little or no movement for the required period. It is also helpful to invite a friend to act as an impartial observer during the presentation so they can confirm your reading of the cat's reactions. The presenter's movements between each test should also be kept to a minimum with the session being conducted in a precise and formal manner. Conversation between presenter and observer should be strictly limited.

3. Make sure your cat has been well fed at least three hours before testing so that hunger responses to the cards are minimized. No other cats or pets should be in the test room and you should ensure that the cat feels at ease with any independent observer who is present. Your cat should not be held, stroked, petted, or talked to during testing and it is most important to

avoid direct eye contact with the cat prior to and during the presentation (see pages 34 & 35).

4. Don't give up too soon. In their early experiments with the test cards, M.O.N.P.A. researchers often found that highly creative cats were slow to respond at first. It sometimes took up to fifty presentations before the cats were able to "see" the images and begin to respond appropriately. However, they warn that, while it pays to be persistent, any more than ten presentations of one image in a day could lead to test sophistication and give ambiguous results.

Further information about cat creativity is available in books such as **Why Cats Paint** by Burton Silver and Heather Busch or on M.O.N.P.A.'s Internet site (see page 4), which features a different cat painting each day along with critical comments and current valuations.

How To Calculate Your Cat's CQ

Use the scoring criteria accompanying each card to find a per-card score, then add all the scores together to calculate your cat's creative quotient or CQ.

0 – 10: Aesthetically Challenged. Cats in this range are unable to respond to any type of creative stimulus or produce any form of art.

11 – 40: Marginally Aware. This group includes cats who are unlikely to produce works of any significance beyond making crude territorially-motivated marks of little, if any, aesthetic value.

41 – 85: Creatively Motivated. Cats in this bracket, while seldom able to produce valuable works, can, over time, be encouraged to use heavily-scented acrylic paints to achieve some interesting effects.

86 – 120: Artistically Adept. These cats are quick to take advantage of any paints or sculptural materials which are left out for them and derive a great deal of stimulation from trips to art galleries and museums. Many internationally recognized cat artists, who earn in excess of $20,000 annually, fall in the upper limits of this percentile.

121 – 160: Highly creative. Cats in this range earn more than $10,000 for a top-quality painting and are often capable of producing two a week.

2D RECOGNITION TEST

This card tests your cat's ability to perceive a two-dimensional image. Dogs, for example, are not able to make sense of flat images like this, but some cats with a high creative quotient (CQ) are. If your cat reacts to the image in some way (see tail position chart), it is a sign that the cat is capable of perceiving a 2D image. This means that it may be capable of constructing representational images as well as exploring feelings through more expressive works. Some cats with a very high CQ may look rapidly from side to side when viewing this image because they are able to see the second, less obvious image of a dog with its nose pointing right. As many artistic felines are highly imaginative, this dual image may suggest to the cat the possibility of a surprise attack and the presenter should be prepared for sudden hissing, spitting, and/or flight. On the other hand, as the primary image is of a dog in victim mode, it may excite uncontrolled paw swiping and the presenter must be ready to withdraw the card quickly in order to avoid injury.

SCORE: 10 points if your cat looks rapidly from side to side when viewing this image. Score 5 points if it exhibits any immediate fear or flight response or 2 points for any defensive or offensive reaction, such as emitting a low yowling noise or sudden paw swiping.

2D RECOGNITION TEST

COLOR COMPOSITION TEST

This card tests your cat's preference for formal or informal color compositions. The shape made by the elements in each composition remains the same but the way the color is distributed creates a different compositional balance. The left-brain dominated cat is more inclined to select (by either sniffing or patting) the symmetrical compositions represented in figs. I, II, & III, while the right-brained creative cat is likely to choose the informal, asymmetrical, and more interesting color balances shown in figs. IV, V, & VI. A cat which shows a preference for the formal compositions may still have potential as an artist, but its works will tend to be classically-based rather than original and avant-garde. Any cat which shows a marked interest in fig. III is likely to be simply responding to the more face-like nature of this design, and you can be fairly certain your pet has a below average CQ.

SCORE: 10 points if your cat consistently sniffs or paws at figs. IV, V, and VI or 5 points if it rubs the side of its head against them. Score 3 points if the cat looks fixedly at the above figs. Add an extra 5 points to the cat's score if, in addition, it adopts tail positions II, III, V, or IX (as shown on page 45) when viewing figs. IV, V, and VI.

COLOR COMPOSITION TEST

fig. I

fig. II

fig. III

fig. IV

fig. V

fig. VI

M.O.N.P.A. CAT CREATIVITY TEST CARD NO: II

Brain Dominance Test

This card tests your cat for right or left brain dominance. If your cat has a preference for the bird on the left-hand side (fig. I), which it may show by sniffing at or touching with its paw, then it is likely to be a more creative right-brained cat. You should repeat this test at least four times within a one-hour period ensuring a consistent response in order to confirm brain dominance. Tail position can also be used as a guide to brain dominance in cats. Non-artistic left-brained cats' tails will generally favor the right side, while the right-brained cat's tail will favor the left (see picture page 34). In order to attract your cat's attention in the initial phase of presentation, high-pitched tweeting noises are permissible. Rapid rubbing of loose clothing to simulate the fluttering of feathers may also assist in the primary arousal stage.

SCORE: 10 points if your cat sniffs or pats fig. I or 5 points if its tail is in the left quadrant (see above) while viewing this image. Score 15 if the cat exhibits both these behaviors simultaneously.

BRAIN DOMINANCE TEST

fig.I   *fig.II*

M.O.N.P.A. Cat Creativity Test Card No: III

INK BLOT TEST

This card tests your cat's ability to appreciate the overall meaning of a design rather than being distracted by the different elements that make up the whole. Cats able to do the former will be better at constructing a coherent work. Disparate elements of interest to the cat with a fragmented bent are (from top): two cats' heads, two dogs' heads, two begging dogs, two turkeys' heads, and a variety of entrails – probably, though not necessarily, related to the animals listed above. The cat which looks rapidly from one part of the image to another, when the card is held 6 inches from its face, is displaying classic fragmentist tendencies and is unlikely to be able to complete coherent designs. On the other hand, a cat which stares fixedly at the image is more likely to appreciate the overall nature of the composition, in this case a representation of a paw print, a rat's skull, or possibly the flattened form of the short-tentacled Carthusian jellyfish, *Siponophora melegris*.

SCORE: 10 points if your cat stares fixedly at the ink blot for a minimum of 15 seconds, or 5 points for a minimum of 7 seconds. Score 3 points if the cat looks sideways at the image for at least 4 seconds.

INK BLOT TEST

M.O.N.P.A. Cat Creativity Test Card No: IV

INCONSISTENCY TEST

This card tests your cat's advanced aesthetic sensibilities by determining whether it reacts to the obvious inconsistency in the pattern. If the cat sniffs at the rabbit, places a paw on it, or uses its more efficient peripheral vision to look at it sideways, it is likely that it registers the inconsistency. This is a sure sign of a cat with an advanced creative potential. However, you should ensure that your cat is not hungry when introduced to this card, as multiple images of live food may override its artistic sensitivity and encourage the cat to react to all the elements of the pattern with equal enthusiasm.

SCORE: 10 points if your cat sniffs at the rabbit, places its paw on it, or licks it. Score 5 points if it looks sideways at the image and 3 points if it adopts a rabbit-like stance while viewing the card.

INCONSISTENCY TEST

M.O.N.P.A. CAT CREATIVITY TEST CARD NO:V

THE PERIPHERAL VISION TEST

This card checks whether your cat uses its peripheral vision and enables you to assess its preferred way of viewing art. Hold the card very close to the cat's face and note whether the cat turns its head to the side to study the image with its more movement-specific peripheral vision. Cats use this vision far more than we realize, which is why they will suddenly look intently in one direction when there seems to us to be nothing there. If the cat checks the card peripherally, it is a sure sign that your pet has little interest in the formal, static image, preferring instead to seek out the more exciting, movement-related aspects of art. Cats with a highly developed creative imagination may stare intently at the focal point of the image and sway their heads from side to side. The head sway enables the cat to use its binocular vision to check the precise distance of an object of prey, and if this behavior is accompanied by a crouched stance you should ensure that your hands are well clear of the target area.

SCORE: 10 points if your cat looks intently at the image and sways its head from side to side. Score 5 if the cat turns its head to the side and studies the image for more than 15 seconds with its peripheral vision. Score 2 if it studies the image peripherally for a minimum of 5 seconds.

PERIPHERAL VISION TEST

M.O.N.P.A. Cat Creativity Test Card No:VI

fig. I

The cards should be held directly in front of, or just below the cat's face (fig. III), rather than from above (fig. I), which can result in a stiff neck for some cats. It is also important to remember that when a cat turns its face away from a card (fig. II), it may not be expressing disinterest but in fact examining the image with its more movement-specific peripheral vision. In this case, the curved tail position tells the presenter that the cat, though slightly annoyed, is still interested. The erect tail signal in fig. III indicates strong positive interest.

fig. II

fig. III

COMPOSITIONAL TEST

This card tests your cat's preference for static or dynamic composition as seen in the two scratch-works on table legs. Cats who show an interest in the single focal-point scratch-form composition (fig. I) will tend to be more formal and conservative in their artistic expression, while those who indicate a preference for the multiple focal-point, movement-oriented composition (fig. II), will create works which take more risks and push the boundaries of artistic expression. Cats with a serious aesthetic impairment often miss the scratch-forms altogether and instead become fixated on the two counterposed leg-forms themselves, patting one and then the other with increasing excitement. One researcher has suggested these cats may be interpreting the forms as animate (or potentially animate) beings such as, "two parrots conversing while seated on round perches." This assumption on the part of a cat, while understandable in the feline-avian prey context, is artistically misguided.

SCORE: 10 points if your cat pats or claws at fig. I in an obvious attempt to alter it. Score 5 points if the cat sniffs at, or rubs its head against, fig. II, or 3 points if its tail is in the right quadrant (see page 12), while looking at the image.

COMPOSITIONAL TEST

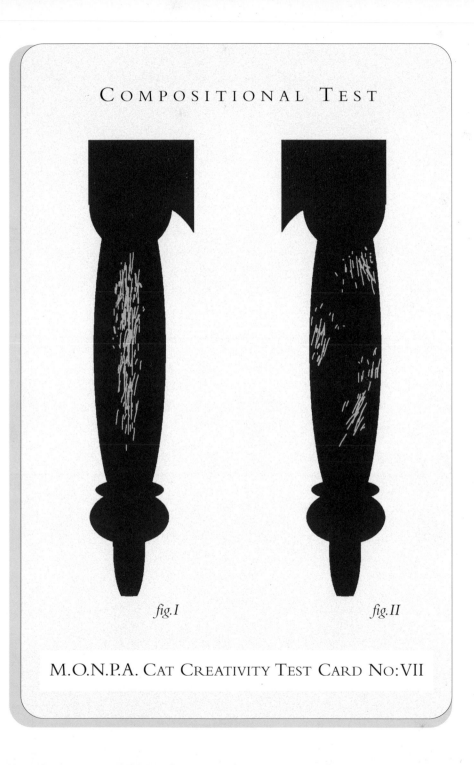

fig.I   fig.II

M.O.N.P.A. CAT CREATIVITY TEST CARD No:VII

COLOR BLINDNESS TEST

This card tests your cat's ability to see color. Many cats have difficulty in differentiating between colors, but cats that paint have been found to have a far more highly attuned color sense. If your cat is able to distinguish between the main color groups it should exhibit a noticeable reaction to the image which, when held upright, shows a highly magnified rear view of the female cat's relevant area when she is in the ready-to-mate position. Inverted, the image depicts a greatly enlarged frontal view of the male cat's relevant anatomical trigger point in the ready-to-mount mode. The image should be viewed in natural light and held at a distance of 4 inches from the line of vision. It is not suitable for kittens.

SCORE: Reactions to this card vary depending on the gender of the cat being tested. Strong reactions for a female cat include rolling around suggestively after viewing the card, or hissing and spitting at it, whereas a male cat may attempt to straddle the card or run in the opposite direction. Strong reactions like these score 10 points. Moderate reactions in a female include purring and rubbing against the card or paw-flicking to indicate distaste. On the other hand, a male may drool in the crouched position or ask to be let out. Reactions like these score 5 points. If a female cat lies down and purrs or turns away and washes herself she is showing a mild reaction, while a male may sniff in the direction of the card or very obviously sniff at some other object. Mild reactions like these score 2 points. This scoring system takes account of the fact that highly creative cats generally have far greater sex drives compared with their less creatively energized peers.

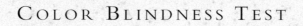

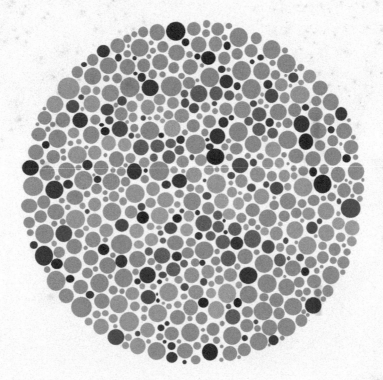

M.O.N.P.A. CAT CREATIVITY TEST CARD NO: VIII

VISUAL DISPLAY TEST

This card tests your cat's appreciation of visual display. It is generally accepted that the more aesthetically inclined a cat is, the more time it will take to carefully arrange its dismembered prey in an attractive manner. The non-creative cat, on the other hand, shows little concern for display and will almost always be more interested in the complete rat depicted at the top of the card, while the cat with a highly developed artistic sense will appreciate the even, symmetrical quality of the attractively displayed parts of rat. If your cat deliberately sniffs at each of the separated elements of the rat it demonstrates an even higher degree of aesthetic appreciation since the individual elements offer new interpretive possibilities. These are (from left): eel, upside-down hen, open-mouthed fish (facing left) or goose (facing right), bird on branch or upside-down bird flying and upside-down owl building a nest.

SCORE: 10 points if your cat deliberately sniffs at each of the separated elements in fig. II. Score 5 points if it simply sniffs, paws, or licks at fig. II and 2 points if it looks fixedly at fig. II for more than 10 seconds.

VISUAL DISPLAY TEST

fig.I

fig.II

M.O.N.P.A. CAT CREATIVITY TEST CARD NO: IX

SINGLE PREFERENCE TEST

This card tests the cat's preference for a single image as opposed to a multiple image which is shown on the next page. Hold the card 6 inches from the cat's face and then quickly turn the page to present the multiple image. Go from one image to the other every two seconds for approximately one minute. This should be sufficient time to tell whether your cat has a preference for the single or multiple image. Most aesthetically mature cats prefer the more interesting repeating pattern of multiple images – though you should ensure your cat has been well fed prior to this test as the multiple image may appeal more to the base instincts of a hungry cat and could lead to an inaccurate reading.

SCORE: 10 points if your cat's pupils suddenly expand on viewing the multiple image and 5 points if its tail becomes fluffed up and fully erect (see page 45) when looking at this image. Score 15 points if the cat exhibits both these behaviors simultaneously.

MULTIPLE PREFERENCE TEST

This card tests the cat's preference for a multiple image as opposed to a single image which is shown on the previous page. Hold the card 6 inches from the cat's face and then quickly turn the page to present the single image. Go from one image to the other every two seconds for approximately one minute. This should be sufficient time to tell whether your cat has a preference for the single or multiple image. Most aesthetically mature cats prefer the more interesting repeating pattern displayed in the multiple image. It is important not to carry out this test in an overly hot or cold environment as the draft caused by the fanning action of turning the pages back and forth may either delight or annoy your cat and result in an incorrect reading.

SCORE: 10 points if your cat's pupils suddenly expand on viewing the multiple image and 5 points if its tail becomes fluffed up and fully erect (see page 45) when looking at this image. Score 15 points if the cat exhibits both these behaviors simultaneously.

MULTIPLE PREFERENCE TEST

M.O.N.P.A. CAT CREATIVITY TEST CARD NO: XI

PATTERN PREFERENCE TEST

This card tests your cat's preference for complex or simple patterns. Once hunger is satisfied, many cats will play with their remaining dry-food kibbles, pushing them into a variety of shapes and patterns. Generally speaking, the more aesthetically minded a cat is, the more complex and interesting patterns it will make. To test your cat, call it, and, as soon as you have its attention, place the card on the ground in front of you. Repeat this at least six times, orienting the card differently each time and carefully noting which pattern the cat sniffs at or touches first. The more visually literate cat will choose fig. II which has four units of repetition as opposed to fig. I which has only one. Alternatively, you can offer your cat two different displays of real food – one laid out in a complex pattern and the other in a non-complex manner. Just as a gourmet, no matter how hungry, will prefer well-presented food, so too the aesthetically inclined cat will be more drawn to a creatively advanced display of cat food rather than an unattractive mess.

SCORE: 10 points if your cat paws or licks at fig. I in an obvious attempt to alter it. Score 5 points if it sniffs repeatedly at different areas of fig. II and 2 points if it simply concentrates on fig. II for a minimum of 10 seconds.

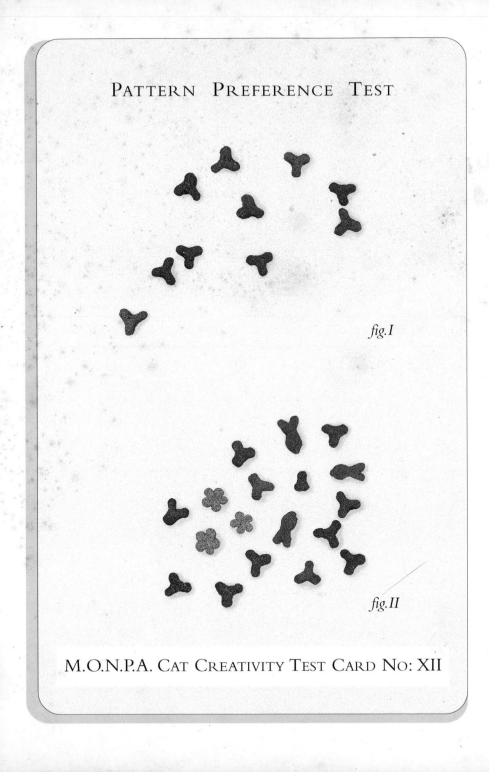

PATTERN PREFERENCE TEST

fig.I

fig.II

M.O.N.P.A. CAT CREATIVITY TEST CARD NO: XII

fig. I

It is important not to stare directly at the cat when presenting a card because this is seen by the cat as a threat and it is likely to feel intimidated and lose interest. However, because the presenter needs to closely examine the cat's reactions it is difficult not to engage in prolonged staring. One way round this is to stand with your back to the cat and use a mirror to watch how the cat reacts (figs. I & II), or alternatively present the card from behind the cat (fig. III).

fig. II

fig. III

INVERTISM TEST

This card tests your cat's preference for inverted or non-inverted objects. Some cats paint simple representations of objects but for some reason render them upside down. These cats often lie on the ground and look at things the wrong way up and may take a sudden and uncharacteristic interest in watching the television when it is turned upside down. If your cat shows a preference for the upside-down fish (fig. II) it is likely to have invertist tendencies, and you should turn its paintings upside down before studying them for clues to possible interpretations.

SCORE: 10 points if your cat sniffs or pats fig. II or 5 points if it rolls onto its back and looks upside down at the inverted image. Score 15 if the cat exhibits both these behaviors.

INVERTISM TEST

fig.I

fig.II

M.O.N.P.A. CAT CREATIVITY TEST CARD No: XIII

SHAPE PREFERENCE TEST

This card tests your cat's preference for different shapes, giving an indication of its likely artistic approach and style. The card should be laid on the floor in front of the cat and careful note should be taken of which image it expresses most interest in. Cats who prefer the upper image (fig. I), which is tightly bound, formal, and controlled, will tend to approach their art methodically. Generally their works will be stylistically conservative and unlikely to push aesthetic conventions. Cats who show greater interest in the random shape (fig. II) will be more expressive, willing to use their work to explore unknown territories, and likely to respond to happy accidents. They will therefore also be more likely to deliberately spill their milk in order to interact with complex shapes and forms.

SCORE: 10 points if your cat sniffs, pats, or licks at fig. II, 5 points if it simply concentrates on fig. II for 10 seconds or more, and 3 points if it uses its more movement-specific peripheral vision to look sideways at either or both images.

SHAPE PREFERENCE TEST

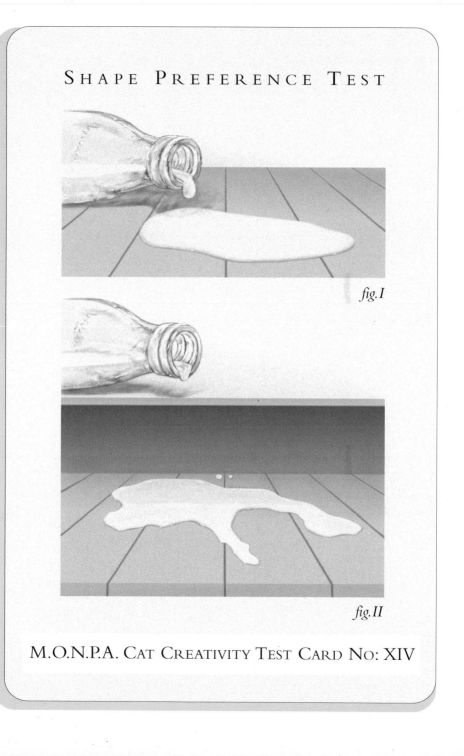

fig. I

fig. II

M.O.N.P.A. Cat Creativity Test Card No: XIV

OPTICAL SENSATION TEST

This card is designed to test how much your cat is affected by optical sensations, and thereby allow you to determine the degree of stimulation it is likely to derive from undertaking a painting or sculptural work of its own. The image should be held 6 inches in front of the cat, and, once it appears to be engaged by the image (look for pupil dilation), the card should be moved slowly round in small concentric circles. If the cat shows any signs of excitement, such as: tail lashing, paw swiping, spasmodic lunging, hissing, biting, sudden vomiting, unsteadiness, or confusion, it almost certainly has a well-developed artistic sense and should derive a great deal of satisfaction from undertaking artworks of various kinds. However, a cat exhibiting any of the first five behaviors outlined above is likely to show a talent for expressive sculptural clawing or chewing and owners are advised to make furniture with soft coverings readily available for appropriation at all times.

SCORE: 10 points if your cat exhibits any examples of pronounced excitement as outlined above and 5 points for the milder forms which include unsteadiness and general confusion. Score 3 points if the cat goes straight to sleep after looking at the image.

OPTICAL SENSATION TEST

M.O.N.P.A. CAT CREATIVITY TEST CARD NO: XV

THE LITTER TRAY TEST

This card shows some of the litter tray paw marks made by artistically able cats. Cats not only rely on the scent of their feces to demarcate their territory but also physically mark its position by carefully "drawing" lines that point towards it like a large arrowhead. Such lines are clearly visible to other cats long after the scent has faded, and act as a kind of signature. If your cat has artistic potential, its signature lines will tend to be quite symmetrically placed (fig. I) or will be typified by regular curved forms of varying complexity (figs. II, III & IV). There are other litter tray behaviors which may indicate your cat has advanced aesthetic sensibilities. These include: (i) the cat wiping the litter tray dust from its paws onto the wall, (ii) spending up to 15 minutes a day contemplating its litter tray marks, (iii) spending up to 30 minutes per day looking at other cats' litter tray marks, (iv) spending even longer studying curved marks you make in its litter tray to encourage it.

THE LITTER TRAY TEST

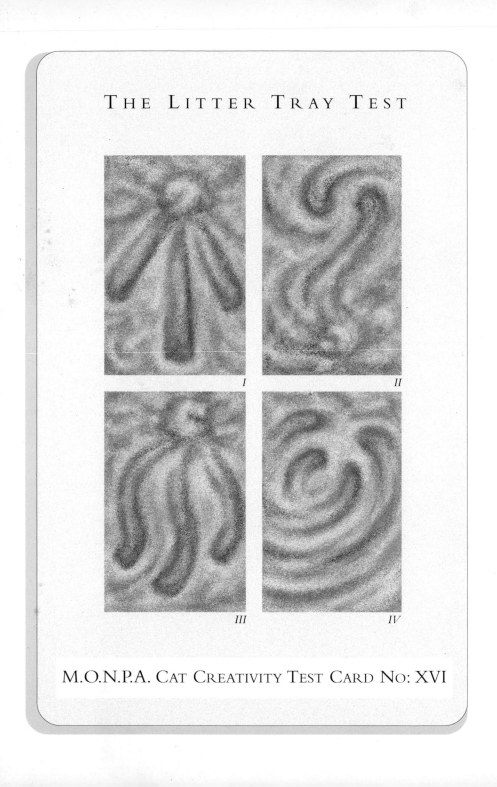

I

II

III

IV

M.O.N.P.A. CAT CREATIVITY TEST CARD NO: XVI

TAIL POSITION CHART

All cats signal their moods with their tails, and this card shows the nine major tail signals to look for when interpreting your cat's interest in the test card images.

I   Flat on ground, slightly curved: moderate interest.

II   Fluffed up and fully erect: strong positive interest.

III Semi-erect, undulating: intermittent interest.

IV Walking away with tail curved slightly upwards: neutral, no interest.

V   Raised and slightly curved inwards: becoming interested.

VI Fluffed up and swishing violently from side to side: extreme negative interest, could result in attack.

VII Walking off, tail fluffed up and well curved over: puzzlement and annoyance, negative interest.

VIII Lowered and forward of hind legs: fear has led to extreme lack of interest.

IX Semi-erect and fluffed up with small flicks of the tip: very interested but also irritated.

TAIL POSITION CHART

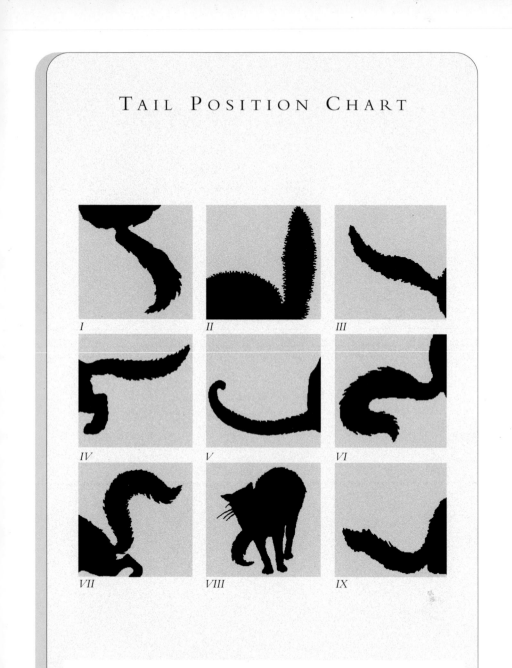

I

II

III

IV

V

VI

VII

VIII

IX

M.O.N.P.A. CAT CREATIVITY TEST CARD No: XVII

COLOR & TONE TEST

This card helps you to check your cat's artistic temperament by demonstrating how some aesthetically aware cats consistently choose the color and tone of the surface they lie on to contrast or harmonize with their fur coloring. An artistically conservative ginger cat for example, will select warm colors to blend in with the yellowish-red of its fur, thereby making it merge in harmoniously with the chair (figs. I & VI) or it may choose a lighter chair (fig. III) which makes its body look darker and recede. On the other hand, an artistically expansive cat will go for contrasting colors which enhance the vibrancy of its fur (figs. II & V) or darker colors which make it look larger and stand out (fig. IV). Aesthetically challenged cats have little understanding of color and tone and often choose to lie on surfaces with colors which do not compliment their personalities. Many such cats who may be quite extroverted show their complete lack of color sense by choosing to sleep on fabrics that harmonize with their fur coloring while some particularly shy cats are frequently so insensitive, they will happily curl up on a contrasting color, blissfully unaware of the way it makes them stand out.

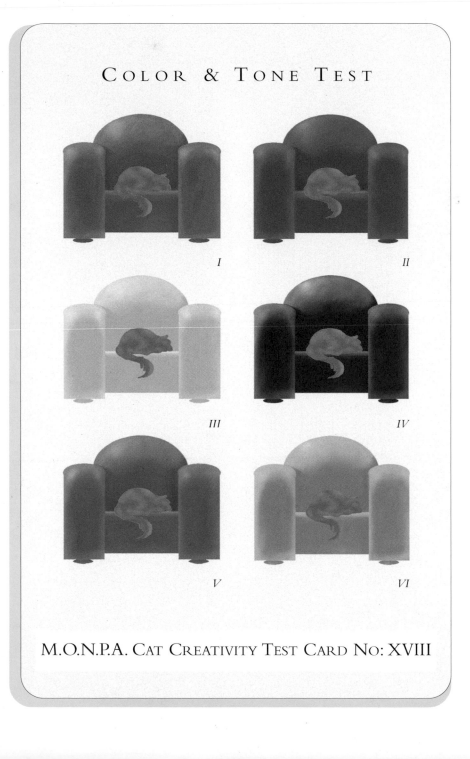

COLOR & TONE TEST

I

II

III

IV

V

VI

M.O.N.P.A. Cat Creativity Test Card No: XVIII

TEN SPEED PRESS
P.O. Box 7123,
Berkeley, California 94707

Text, illustrations, and photographs © 1996,
Conclusion Trust.

Published in association with the Museum of Non-Primate Art (M.O.N.P.A.).

Neither the publisher, author, or illustrator accept any responsibility for adverse reactions
which may result from the use of any material in this book. In this regard it is advised
that Test Card XV should not be presented to guinea pigs or hamsters and
Card VIII should under no circumstances be shown to albino rabbits.

Library of Congress Catalog information is on file with the publisher.

ISBN 0 - 89815 - 879 - 6

Original card design and book layout: Melissa da Souza-Correa.
Editing: Bronwen Wall.

Compiled and produced by Silverculture Press,
487 Karaka Bay Rd, Seatoun, Wellington 3,
New Zealand.

Page Two:
MINDLE & MOITLE (left), *Swinging Swallows*, 1994.
Scented acrylic on card, 48 x 68cm.
Private Collection, New York.

First printing 1996

Printed and bound in Hong Kong

1 2 3 4 5 - 00 99 98 97 96